UNTITLED, 2004

a poem

After Hours Editions
New York • Kingston
afterhourseditions.com

Cover design and artwork by Eric Amling
Typesetting: Guy Pettit
Editors: Sarah Jean Grimm & Eric Amling

Library of Congress Control Number: 2020933090

First edition
ISBN-978-1-7334082-2-6

After Hours Editions are distributed by Small Press Distribution

Printed on recycled acid-free paper

FSC www.fsc.org MIX Paper from responsible sources FSC® C011935

UNTITLED, 2004

a poem

LAWRENCE
GIFFIN

AFTER
HRS
editions

for Agnes Giffin

October 12 or 15, the twelfth
surely, certainly 2016 that I know,
your mother and I took the train
uptown to see the Agnes Martin
retrospective at the Guggenheim,
and still a year and change before your birth,
we hadn't thought of naming you Agnes
and wouldn't until your mother was
well into her pregnancy with you.
Shakespeare's wife Ann was born
Agnes Hathaway, back when
people thought Agnes was just
a version of Anna, which is not,
like Agnes, from the Greek but comes instead
from the Hebrew meaning "grace."
It had only been a month since she'd
miscarried after our first try,
the two of us staring together
at the plum-sized yolk sac limp
in her hand like a brown jellyfish,
unable to reconcile the image
of our short-lived fantasy
with the formless membrane
that in an uncanny fog we found
too sad not to flush down the toilet.
In its place, we get to have
the awkward joy of having you
instead (talk about "grace,"
to be born and live), though

your beginning was no less
bloody—as all beginnings are—
so much so that it's hard to connect
cute, little you to the senseless
misery that attended your birth.
And don't let it get to you, we are
all here in somebody's place, and
that goes too for those whose place we take.
Like Tristram Shandy's mother
interrupting his father in
medias res to ask if he'd
remembered to wind the clock,
so many accidents attended
each of our conceptions.
Of course, for you, this otherwise
abstract notion had a very
concrete manifestation,
but to paraphrase a line from Auden,
it doesn't take a grave,
to prove the child ephemeral.

The trouble with beginnings is
they never take place quite at the
beginning. I feel this most intensely
when I lay you in your crib and watch
you eye, with what I take to be
wonder, your mobile's paper barn
swallows, trying to imagine what
mindless urge is motivating you,
how you expect the world to be,
and how you think you fit in it.

Why should your world be to me
so alien, so opaque?
Was I not once an infant, too,
and relatively recently, at that?
Still, nothing recognizably
from that time for me remains.
A beginning falls in the middle of
something already in progress—
no doubt a familiar notion to you,
born in the month named for the god
of both beginnings and endings,
portals, pergolas, and overpasses—
and what must give way is never
eager to take its bow and vainly
stride off into an oblivion
that can but be forgotten.

When Agnes Martin was eighty-one,
she left her home in Galisteo,
New Mexico, which she had built
about sixteen years earlier,
and moved into an assisted-
living facility in Taos.
She lived there for eleven years
before she died at ninety-two,
on the 16th of December
2004. The Taos Pueblo,
just north of the city, has been
inhabited continuously
for nearly a millennium.
So much for "our ancestors

taming the continent," as Trump
declared today, exhorting those
he addressed not to apologize
but "to stand up for America,"
mere days after the NFL
announced it would force players
to stand for the national anthem.
In 1660, the residents of the pueblo
burned down the Catholic Church built there
forty years before and killed its priest,
doing the same again in 1680,
after it had been rebuilt
(two priests that time),
during what is now referred to as
the Pueblo Revolt, a combined assault
on the colonists by more than two
dozen pueblos up and down
the Rio Grande Valley,
which drove out the Spanish
and kept them out for twelve years.

In Walter Benjamin's fable
in which the angel of history
is unable to return
to paradise, pinned to the sky
by a storm that blows from that
very place of return (which
turns out is just the offal heap
outside of history's
automated slaughterhouse),
the question is never posed

whether the angel could yet
turn away, abandon the
uncomely remains
of his former home
and instead ascend?
Or having neared the apex of
his unwilled trajectory,
suspended in the interval
between a question never asked
and a reply never to come,
will he tumble down into
the heart of the catastrophe? Agnes,
I'm half-afraid, half-glad the world
explicitly will be for you
what it is still secretly
for us, one emptied of the chance
for redemption, a garden
where a person wouldn't know
of any other use for a ploughshare.
The music of paradise is made
of the continual clashing of swords.
The storm which detains the angel
is named "progress," and I can't help
but hear in Benjamin's choice of this name
a sense that the messiah will be
a global intrusion of cockroaches.

It's just like me
to start at the end of the world
(though what is a beginning if
it does not, in beginning itself,

end another's world), so much
anxiety about how to embark
when I could just begin somewhere
as explicit as the moment of
your conception in a petri dish,
for which we have the time,
right down to the second, in fact,
when zinc was expelled with a spark
from the newly formed embryo which
we've since taken to calling "Agnes."
But aren't your origins more
circumstantial than the chemical bonding
of genetic material? Aren't we all,
Shandy-like, the fallout of
innumerable accidents beyond
all control, much less ours? Or am I just
bringing Sterne back in to stall,
since the point at which I chose
to start this poem, Martin's retrospective,
was chosen arbitrarily by
some power not my own, a deep,
unconscious wish from which
the lines that follow will attempt
to fabricate some significance,
and not entirely disingenuously,
just like some future Roach Christ will
try to divine a meaning from
the end of human civilization
merely by its writhing across
the face of the earth.
And so, *Shandy*-like, I'll return

to that time before you were
even a loping homunculus,
and tell you a little about
some Agnes Martin paintings
and about painting in general,
about death and the problem of origins,
about forms of nondestructive
and uninstrumentalizable negativity,
about ancient pueblo ruins,
the Baroque (particularly its
landscapes), early Industrial Age
tourism, Kabbalah (weirdly),
and everything that's in between.
Can you tell that I'm still stalling? I
just can't seem to bring myself to say,
"With all that said, should we begin?"

*

At the retrospective, we got a sense
of the evolution of Martin's work
from the paintings of the 1960s,
which are dominated by
the grid, to those from the mid-1970s on,
which are almost exclusively
made up of horizontal bands.
In an interview from 1976, Martin
describes her discovery of
the vertical dimension,
inextricably bound up
with her discovery of the

horizontal: "One time, I was
coming out of the mountains,
and having painted the mountains,
I came out on this plain and thought,
Ah! What a relief!
The expansiveness of it.
I sort of surrendered. This plain
was just like a straight line.
And I thought there wasn't a line that
affected me like a horizontal line.
Then, I found that the more I
drew that line, the happier
I got. First I thought it was like
the sea, then, I thought it was like
singing! But I didn't like it
without any verticals.
And I thought to myself,
there aren't too many verticals I like.
But I did put a few in there.
Finally, I was putting in
almost as many verticals
as horizontals." Her discovery
of the horizontal is
overshadowed immediately by
that of the vertical and the grid,
the abstract space
of the mountain's slope, rise over run.
It would be nearly two decades
before she rediscovered that
horizontal line "like the sea,"
"like singing," recovering that

initial feeling of surrender
and expansiveness that struck her
with uncoordinated relief.
Her rediscovery of the horizontal
follows her seven-year break
from painting (from 1967
to 1974). In
the earlier period, the
paintings consist mostly of rigid,
ruler-made grids over paint applied
in uneven bands or on top of crude,
single-color swaths in variegated
or expressive strokes and rough textures.
Sometimes, the grid appears on top
of bare canvas, its rough warp and weft
a counter to the clean and rigid grid,
popped threads or snags running ragged
between cleanly crossing lines,
or in the negative space between
rectangular sections of gold leaf.

In these early works, there is a tension
between the predictability
and regularity of the grid
and the rough wildness of
texture, tone, and stroke,
a tension which seems to dominate
the first period of Martin's work,
though I wouldn't have thought as much
if I hadn't been able to see
the early works hung next to those

made after her break from painting,
during which she built two adobe
houses and a log cabin.
When she returned to painting, her
form had changed. She said, "It took me
a great intensity of work
to find out that I had to give
up the symmetrical." The grid had been
abandoned in favor of parallel
lines, at first only vertical lines
but then almost exclusively
horizontal lines drawn parallel
in pencil, filled in with bands
mostly of pastel washes, which
became her signature style.
In this period, colors stay within the lines,
and the brush strokes, while still
of slightly varying consistency,
run parallel to them,
like atoms falling in the void.
Here is an order that is not
that of the grid struggling
against the chaos of the paint,
nor the "contradiction" and
"dissonance" she saw between
the grid's rectangles and the square
canvas, "destroying its power."
The tension is gone.
The vertical is mostly abandoned.
Here there is a harmony between
line and figure, texture and abstraction,

rule and irregularity.
Strokes are usually a
standard width (that of the brush),
each applied with only slightly
varying pressure.

Martin herself was aware of a shift
in her work after the '67–
'74 break. She wrote,
"Painting is not about
ideas or personal emotion
When I was painting in New York
I was not so clear about that
Now I'm very clear
that the object is freedom." But
this decisive declaration
is contradicted, I think,
by her final painting, *Untitled,*
2004, which hung,
at the retrospective, alone in
an alcove at the end of the
Guggenheim's immense spiral.
This painting comprises six
horizontal bands,
four dark gray and two of a lighter shade.
The pigment is unevenly applied,
which is unusual for her work.
The dark grays resemble storm clouds or
sheets of rain. On its own it's
a striking work, but especially so
in contrast to her entire career,

which your mom and I had both
just surveyed in abbreviated form.
I came to this last painting
before she did, and though I find
the public performance of rapturous
ecstasy before art disingenuous
(especially in regards to non-
figurative art), I could
hardly suppress a shiver myself,
coming upon what appeared to be
a refutation of a life's work,
and I looked forward to
seeing your mother's reaction,
which I felt, regardless of what
I think about that sort of thing,
would be fully justified.
And when we left, she was
the happiest I think I'd ever seen her,
sitting in a booth at the Lexington
Candy Shop having an egg cream.

*

A year or so before you were born
(the summer before the Guggenheim),
your mother and I took a road trip through
New Mexico and Arizona,
the landscape sometimes flat desert,
an eyeful of black, red, and green mesas,
rising up from cloud-like taluses,
other times rolling grassland or

thick stands of aspen or ponderosa.
My eye could never quite fix on any
element of these landscapes; the moment
my gaze zeroed in on something,
some rock or bush, my eye
would already have moved elsewhere,
to the surrounding rocks
in the same talus deposit and then
have followed it to the point of its cone,
which seemed to pour from a long
vertical fissure eroded into the side of the mesa,
itself stretching back to the hazy horizon,
nearly unobscured, so that before
I could really take in the initial
individual rock or bush,
I was right back at the panorama,
though even that panorama
decayed into an incoherence whose
unity was only a function of
the limits of my vision.

The abortive details in nature,
which are only ever half formed,
appearing only then to be shuttled
along their own lines of flight
like Jane Crofut's home address
(the leaf, the tree, the forest, mountain,
sky, Earth, galaxy, universe),
are avoided in the depiction of
nature in landscape painting,
not merely because every detail is

in focus, but also through the use,
particularly in the seventeenth
and eighteenth centuries,
of something called "staffage,"
miniature depictions of
people engaged in sundry outdoorsy
activities: picnicking, frolicking,
sneaking off to semi-private clearings,
herding sheep or oxen,
giving chase to prey, or even
acting out a Biblical scene:
the expulsion from Eden, the
exodus from Egypt,
the escape from Sodom with
its telltale pillar and ashen pleasures.

Different from rural or pastoral scenes,
such as those found, for instance,
in Brueghel's work, in which
people and their activities
are the focus, these figures in Baroque
landscapes are subordinate
and peripheral to the depiction of
the natural environment.
Their technical term, "staffage," is
a pseudo-French formation of
a German word for "ornament," itself
borrowed from the Middle French
estoffer, meaning to garnish,
and where we get our English word 'stuff'.
Although the word was not in use

until the eighteenth century,
first in German and then in English,
as a concept it has been around at least
since the Flemish painter Karel van
Mander first wrote about these
subordinate vignettes, which he
called *storykens,* or "little stories,"
in his 1604 *Schilder-Boeck.*
As a category, staffage also
includes domestic animals
and beasts of burden and even
buildings and other human-
made structures in the scene,
so long as they are
sufficiently peripheral:
a lone turret or mouldering priory,
a hazy bridge, anchored boats
dotting the far-off harbor,
a dusky and vacant hermitage.

Failing to fix one's eye on any one thing
in the natural landscape of the
American Southwest, with its
lack of actually existing staffage,
one tries instead to take the view
entirely as a single unit, only to see
that nature never presents itself
as a single whole. Composed neither
of discrete units nor itself a unity,
nature appears as a mass of contours
barely this side of formlessness

and can only be conceived
as a sum which does not totalize
its own elements. The whole one views
is a mass without perspective without
the organizing vantage point built in
as it is in a landscape by Corot
or Claude Lorrain. And so nature
absconds as if to say,
there is no nature without staffage.

I had the same feeling on that same trip
looking at Martin's paintings
at the Harwood in Taos, walking with
your mother around the octagonal room
designed to display them. Of course,
Martin's paintings aren't landscapes,
at least not in the conventional sense
(although she did ascribe the origin
of her style to the Great Plains).
There is no single detail that catches
the eye—her works are devoid of detail.
Once she even described her paintings
as "anti-nature," but in their minimalism,
they resist our interrogations
in a way not unlike how nature resists.
A resistance in the name of nothing,
which seems to me a lot like nature
in that it too refuses to hide itself. In
an interview from 1977, Martin
said that, like nature, her paintings are
about "formlessness" and about "a world

without objects, without interruption."
The work just is this resistance.
Its content is the specific form
taken by a formal refusal,
which keeps it from becoming
that total and all-encompassing
negativity we find
in the obsessive defenses
of angry young men. To resist at all,
it has to appear, and to appear
at all, it has to appear as
something. Why then not as a landscape?

Martin was open about
the inspiration for her style,
writing, "I used to paint mountains here
in New Mexico and I thought
my mountains looked like ant hills
I saw the plains
driving out of New Mexico
and I thought the plain had it
just the plane.
When I draw horizontals
you see this big plane
and you have certain feelings
like you're expanding over the plane"
So "landscape" may be pushing it
(though, notice how cleanly
she shifts from plain with an 'i'
to plane with an 'e'),
but for a painter who wrote

that "painting is not about ideas
or personal emotion," it's odd
that many of her paintings bear
titles like *Friendship, Innocence,*
Love, Lovely Life,
Ordinary Happiness,
Perfect Day, and *Playing*
(the titles of all the paintings
hanging in the Harwood), and
unless you know a good reason
why such abstract concepts should take
the form of horizontal bars
in desert blues and pinks, we'd do
just fine sticking to calling them "landscapes."

Every painting says more than it means
or means more than it says, which is
its best quality, or its worst
if you are trying to say something specific,
like, *Death is here in paradise, too,* or
The seaside makes everything dreamy.
The subject of a painting, what is
depicted, is put there in the first place
to distract the viewer from
the painting's giddy ambiguity.
For this reason, a painting can never
truly be a patriotic symbol or
a vessel for moral instruction or
an occasion for the worship of a deity
or the undying likeness of
the lord of the estate.

It remains unfinished, which is not
to mean that it says something other than
or even the opposite of
what it seems to say. It only means
that perfected depiction is tragic,
for as Martin noted, "perfection
is unobtainable and unattainable,"
and any critical appendix
just goes the wayward way of Oedipus.
It can, for this reason, say more or less
but it always speaks its tragic flaw.
Martin's work includes this same
incompleteness but minus
the desire to depict. Scraped clean
of content, what remains is the
inconsolable drive to make manifest,
what the Greek philosophers
called *physis,* their word
for the reckless urge of natural things,
akin to our word "to bloom."
That Martin's paintings bear the breadth
of a unique and notable style does not
contradict this notion that
in representing very little,
almost nothing, disconsolation
is made plain and not obscured,
since pictorial accuracy
alienates, exposing all painting
to endless variation.

*

The basic principles of construction
of the ancient pueblo in Aztec, NM,
spoke to the meaning the gone
inhabitants had entertained
with their surroundings,
everything arranged just so
to bring elements of the landscape—
a nearby rock outcropping, the
creek bed, the paths of the sun and
the moon—out from their furtive form-
lessness and into a kind of constellation,
as if nature were part architect,
a configuration so unlike that
of, say, where I am from:
a quantified mass of abstract parcels
on record at the county tax office,
formed like alluvial deposits by flows
of commerce along interstates spilling
into a grid of arterial roads, feeding
the precarious ecosystem of truck stop,
strip mall, distribution center,
eroding the fanciful kinship structures
the old masters had bequeathed,
a muggy delta of sloughed value
whose one dream was to become
the path of least resistance
for merchandise passing from port
to port. But this is no less a meaning.
What could this son
of containerization
make of these ruins?

In their uncanny ancientness,
their departed intimacy was
more present than the bored siblings
touring the site, trying to push
each other off of crumbling walls,
but they were equally tourist traps
on the level of tin UFOs in Roswell,
so that our being herded into
the simulacrum of
the Great Kiva at Aztec,
a re-creation of the pueblo's
sacred communal hearth space, was as much
the manufactured enjoyment of
a cynical Disneyland
of violent dispossession
as a chance to salvage
some meaning from
this abandoned village at
the very moment
my own meaninglessness
was underlined.
To recover the ruin as ruin,
being careful not
to mistake lack of meaning
for meaning's destruction,
like some pale, pimply,
pedantic Hamlet
dominating the seminar
room, claiming for himself
the expiating negativity
that will soon instead

claim him, as if
one could hitch their
historical identity
to entropy's universal
indifference.

Instead, to settle into
the sense of a common
share in powerlessness
as the beginning
of something new that
still might not be
a beginning
(Martin said her paintings
were "about impotence"),
a powerlessness that
finds its beatification
in being very little,
almost nothing, being oneself
barely more than
an avatar of ideology
touring these ruins but more
than, all the same. Their meaning,
which I vainly tried to salvage,
had already withdrawn.
They stood there,
staring me down,
but any interrogation
was fruitless, and it turns
out that was their gift.

*

Along the river Wye, on
the border of England and Wales,
Thomas Gray, the famous "Graveyard
poet" of the eighteenth century,
mounts a prospect where a few
other sightseers are perched,
overlooking the famed Abbey,
whereupon he turns his back
and produces from the pocket of his coat
a thin leather pouch, within which
is what his friend the poet
William Mason would describe
as, "a Plano-convex Mirror
of about four inches diameter
on a black foil, and bound up like
a pocket-book." A Claude glass,
also called a black mirror,
which could be used to gaze on stunning
vistas from romantic prospects by
facing away and viewing the sights
over your shoulder in the glass.
The glass is convex, so
sizes, ranges, and distances are
exaggerated while the colors are
subdued by the smoky mirror.
The resulting reflection would resemble
a landscape by the famed Baroque
painter Claude Lorrain, thus its name.
"Another bourgeois invention

like the piano," as Auden
wrote of the Lake District.

Popularized in early bestsellers
of the burgeoning genre of travel
writing and part and parcel of
the new popular pastime of tourism,
the glass represents nature as
always already alienated
and sentimentalized. The Reverend
William Gilpin mounted one in his
carriage, as if the passing landscape
could only be enjoyed
as the dream of that landscape, as if
nature as such could be recognized
only at the moment that
the natural world became something
set apart, something unreal,
and even then it had to take
the form of a dream or a work of art.
Or as a memory receding into the past.
Nature here appears as something lost,
something one takes down from a shelf
in an antique mall,
smiling at it nostalgically,
but in the end replacing.
We see it only behind us
as in a Claude glass, the
"sweet vision of boyish hours
free as spring clouds and wild
as summer flowers," to quote John

Clare. The sweetness of the vision is
the bitterness of our common
expulsion which affords us it, viewed
either from newly enclosed fields
or from rapidly industrializing towns.
The frame of the glass and its coal-smoky mirror
gives us nature as what was once
that whose "only bondage was
the circling sky" (Clare, again)
but bondage nonetheless.
Something similar took place
in America in the late nineteen-tens
as the number of people
living in cities began
to outnumber those living in rural areas,
the advent of Country music.
"Senility is looking back
with nostalgia," Martin claimed.
When some mouldering priory is
no longer continuous with the landscape,
when a cultural identity
asserts itself at the moment it is
materially degraded, when,
temples, images, and customs are
no longer capable of taking on
the historical vocation of a people
in order to compel it in a new task,
they enter the frame of a black mirror.

*

On our way to Taos,
we pulled off the highway
near Galisteo and found
Martin's second adobe house,
which she had built a decade after
leaving New York.
The first adobe house she built,
on Mesa Portales,
southwest of Cuba, NM,
was too hard to locate.
We could only find the address
for the one in Galisteo
because it was listed for sale
on a real-estate website.

We approached the house
on a small, winding road
flanked by coyote fences
and short adobe walls
with small wooden doors
that opened right onto the road.
Pinyon pines stretched up
over the walls, forming a canopy
over the road,
which ended at the driveway
to Martin's house.
We felt creepy going any farther,
so we drove back out
onto the highway
and pulled over at the curve
that overlooked

the simple house.

I wouldn't say you were named for
Martin, only that the name Agnes
served to mark the promise
of those early days, when
everything that had gone before
willy-nil toward an indefinite future
was roughly abridged into
a prefatory note hastily
scribbled in anticipation
of what was sure to come after.
Now we live in the relief
of waking from the nightmare where
you are yet to be born, which itself
was a nightmare, medically induced,
expectant joy debrided
into merciful deliverance.
Survival was the strait gate
through which you crammed
the contents of our world
compressed into an age-old name.

*

In *Untitled, 2004,*
the washed-out pastels that had
become Martin's trademark since
the 1970s are replaced by
bands of light and dark gray.
The horizontal pencil lines are there,

but the brush strokes are chaotic,
no longer parallel to
the pencil lines (though really
the paint is more spilled than brushed on),
and here and there, a wash
of dark or light gray
crosses the faint boundaries made
in graphite. In this manner, the linearity
of the desert pastels has given way
to wave-like washes spreading over
the canvas like ink on paper
on which water was spilled,
rendering whatever was
written there illegible,
or like waves, like the sea, like
the dark face of the waters
over which the spirit of God moved
in the second verse of *Genesis*.
Mayim, "waters," often a
euphemism for piss or semen,
connoting abundance and danger
(life is later destroyed by
the *mayim* of the flood).
Tohu wa bohu, the priestly author
wrote, formless and empty
(or as we say in our own *Maariv*
"Goodnight nobody / Goodnight mush").
Tohu shares its root with *tahah*,
meaning "to gaze in wonder, confusion,"
and *bohu* with *bahah*, meaning
"a glassy-eyed, vacant stare." In short,

both words mean to be stupefied,
rendered senseless, awed by a void.
So, the phrase *tohu wa bohu* means
not so much "chaos and disorder,"
as it means instead that nothing
presents itself to the gaze,
nothing is there to catch the eye.
There is both too much to take in,
wonder and confusion, and
too little to see, absolute
featurelessness.
"The face of the deep,"
al-pene tehom, disclosing
the hidden as hidden,
zone of indistinction
between surface and depth.
In *Genesis* 1:2, *Élohim* is itself
the very space held open
between two faces (*pene* is grammatically plural),
face of the surface and face of the depths,
countenance and inner life,
and also, maybe, cause and effect.
And *Élohim* is also plural,
forming a space that is never
finally secured, an incongruence
between the two surfaces, such
that they never balance but become
a maelstrom, spiraling endlessly,
returning not to itself but to the accident
from which the Earth itself issues, its
did-not-have-to-be which does not wither.

This erratic style of painting is not only
uncharacteristic of Martin's work,
but she was explicitly opposed to such
a lack of subtlety and uniformity.
Arne Glimcher, who manages
Martin's estate, recalls helping
the aging painter destroy canvases
with which she was not satisfied:
"When I once asked her why she was
destroying a particularly delicate
and beautiful work, she said,
'It's too aggressive, and there's a
mistake'. Most often that referred
to a pooling of colour that made
the brushstrokes discontinuous.
The mistake became an unwanted
'focus', which disturbed its serenity."
Not a single brushstroke in *Untitled, 2004,*
could be called "continuous."
There are hardly any brushstrokes at all,
only pooling grays. The center
of the painting appears
to be two contiguous bands
of the same dark gray, but where
we expect the pencil line to demarcate
a division between upper and lower bands,
the paint spreads across the faint line
as if it were one single block of gray,
ignoring this central division, which before
would have been a stylistic heresy.

But what is most surprising is
the irregular splotch of paint
at the right edge of the canvas,
an unwanted focus that should
not be. Is this irregular splotch
a form of staffage, a minor detail that
frames the painting from within?
Staffage often appears off
to one side, near the edge
of the canvas. The splotch, as a
sort of *hapax graphomenon,*
organizes around it not only the few
elements of *Untitled, 2004,*
but all of Martin's other paintings as well,
the painting itself taking its place
at the edge of her life's work
as a splotch on her dominant style.
I hesitate even to call the splotch
a mistake, since it appears she had
always destroyed any previous
painting with a mistake in it.
The splotch stands out not only from
the painting, then, but from her style
entirely, functioning thus
as the style's own self-
consciousness, as the fulcrum
on which her entire career
pivots back on itself. It's
as if her seven-year break from
painting and the accompanying
break in her style is referenced

in this splotch, which becomes
a sign of that difference between
the tension of the early works
and the harmony of the later ones.

Very near the end of her life,
Martin had Glimcher go into
her studio, again to destroy
some unfinished paintings,
but to leave the one painting
still hanging on the wall untouched.
The two paintings that he destroyed
he called, "absolutely perfect."
I'll let you guess what work was spared.
One wonders if this last painting
is thus a deliberate break with
the formal pattern that had been
established since the seventies,
or if it's simply due to the fact
that her ability as a painter was failing
as she neared the end of her life,
as if this final painting could
be something other than a repudiation.
And though that is entirely
possible, it is contradicted by
Glimcher's recollection that the two
paintings she had him destroy
were very much in the style of
those made on her return to painting,
which would suggest that she was still
able to produce precise minimal works.

And that's not taking into account
the precision of the few, faint
graphite lines in the final work,
suggesting that neither her sight
nor her motor skills were failing her,
and video from the early 2000s
shows her methodically at work,
in control and shockingly so,
her paintbrush smoothly following
the line, barely touching its
imperceptible outer edge. Perhaps
then, the painting is
a deliberate meditation on death,
a sudden pessimism about what's
to come, so uncharacteristic
of her other paintings with
their cheery titles like, *I Love*
the Whole World, Happy Holiday,
and *Faraway Love.*

*

The baskets we saw at the
Wheelwright Museum, in
Santa Fe, woven by Jicarilla
Apache women, are made
of long spirals of willow and sumac
woven with wider
and flatter bands
whose dyed designs
coupled with the spiral foundations

produced a sense of movement in
the baskets themselves,
so that they seemed to be
filling and draining indefinitely,
moving perpetually in their stillness,
each one a self-contained whirlpool.

And like the ruins, they too said "No"
to my searching gaze, and so
as with Martin's paintings
in the Harwood and the Guggenheim,
I turned back toward myself,
rounding the bend in myself
where my responsibility ends
and something else takes over,
perhaps that same anesthetic force
that leaves none left laughing last,
that is to say death's end.
Like rounding a corner
in our neighborhood
to see your mother
waddling toward me,
nearly nine months
along, on her way
to find froyo in December,
and you just lounging
in ninety-eight-degree waves
as if you were a million miles
from snowy Brooklyn
and not just a few
fleshy inches from the shit

we were trying to force you into,
wanting to meet you so bad that we
were willing to strand you here.

Maybe you sensed as much.
You were difficult to coax out.
But there are some beautiful things here
worth seeing and doing,
things that little primate you
were built for and by. That's why
you belong here. You have
nowhere else to go. A force
has caught you up
in its tireless movement,
but in doing so,
it has already released you,
not to return but slowly to unravel
toward a different abyss than the one
from which you were drawn, though
for all intents and purposes
indistinguishable and equally
undesirable. Martin wrote
a little poem that goes,
"The ocean is deathless
The islands arise and die
Quietly come, quietly go
A silent saying breath."
Except the ocean isn't deathless,
and one day, billions of years hence,
after even years are no more,
nothing will ever be said again,

never an again again.
Life is not a circle, Agnes, but a spiral,
like the helix of a conch-shell core,
a circle that just missed
becoming one with itself. There
are baskets in this world that women
have been making continuously
for thousands of years
and which have been filling up
and draining for just as long,
longer even, and having been
turned away by them,
I'm not sure I made it back
to myself in one piece.
Something of them
came back with
me, or something of me
stayed behind with them,
so that the equation doesn't
zero out but is pulled
out of joint by a remainder.

The spiral is the naturally
occurring pattern which requires
the least amount of energy
to produce and maintain,
and some describe eddies,
gyres, and whirlpools in terms
usually reserved for organic life:
self-sustaining, negentropic,
heat dissipating,

persistent and homeostatic,
and even self-replicating,
though in a very qualified way.
The various trash vortexes
in the five major
ocean gyres across the planet,
swirling concentrations
of human-made garbage
(referred to euphemistically as
"marine litter"), are perhaps organisms
that will one day become
sentient maelstroms
of sludge and microplastics,
and maybe you will
get to meet one of them.

*

Boredom is the desire for desire,
desire at its purest and so also,
strangely, at its most empty.
Not exactly the loss of desire
since desire is also wanting,
but as blank hope, in the sense
that Martin wrote, "Without hope there
is still hope. And without desire
there is still hope," a patience
approaching an intolerable
achiness, never acute
but flattening all of creation in
the shadowless light

of an overcast Sunday evening,
so that all the little baubles and souvenirs
bravely supporting time's great wheel—
the books carefully selected and
displayed, the pictures from magazines
clipped and pasted to the wall,
the bath mat chosen for its off-kilter
green, the Ikea sideboard dragged
across a decade of apartments,
the bright Dutch oven adding color
to the bland counter where it sits
unused—all of them become
in this flat glow
oppressively colorless,
flaunting their arbitrariness
as low-grade dread. Boredom is
a lack of future as it otherwise
appears in the guise of
inevitability, and
idling in the nowhere
between what's done and what has yet
to begin—a time when we are,
according to Sontag, "learning
new modes of attention"—we are
allotted the free time to discover
(though often to our own horror)
what might now capture our attention
which could not before. But so often
we run to data-driven solutions
which at the very least engage
us in the activity,

purposive but without purpose,
of scrolling through the feeds. And so,
chafed by the dull buzz of it,
I changed the Durham zip code on
my dating profile to the generic one
Google Maps gave for Brooklyn,
which just so happened to abut
your mother's at the time,
while she just so happened to have
already planned a trip that coming
August across North Carolina,
from the mountains to the sea,
agreeing after a flurry of emails
to make a pit stop in Durham.
It would not be a simple thing,
I thought, to occupy this big-
city academic with
only the cultural odds-and-ends
of the provinces at my disposal.
Here are some artworks that I
dragged her in front of:
a small canvas by Martin,
Untitled #10, 1994;
a floating, womb-like ball
of aluminum foil by Mike Kelley
with a ragged hole opening
onto a red-lit interior;
a copy by Sherrie Levine
of a sculpture by Brancusi of
a newborn, only black instead of white;
a big Katz and a little Albers; one

of those Nick Cave soundsuits;
and an enormous outdoor maze
by Patrick Dougherty
of arching whorls of plaited maple
and sweetgum saplings, mirroring
your mother's curls as she walked
through it naming unseen birds
whose calls filtered in.

I walk through museums, Agnes,
like I walk through the mall:
purposeless loafing, letting the
fantasies on offer move in
and out of my consciousness
like curtains in an open window.
And like the mall, the museum is
the place where I
am always distracted from
what is on display
by a persistent anxiety
to which I find myself
constantly referred, an anxiety
specifically about what I
should be doing in this place.
Assailed by suppositions,
I wonder what am I supposed
to think about what I see, or
really, what am I supposed to be
seeing? Where am I supposed
to stand? And above all, of course,
What is it supposed to mean?

Sontag said that the appeal
to interpretation "sustains
the fancy that there really is
such a thing as the content of
a work of art." The perceived
deficiency of reality
implicit in such "fancy"
suggests that interpretation is
a cover for aggression
and murderous frustration,
"the revenge of the intellect
upon the world." But still,
as Schuyler wrote of his
penchant for naming
flowers in his poetry,
"the temptation
to show off—to
make a show
of knowing more,
than, in fact, I
know, is very real."

Desire is the thing, Agnes,
that makes a difference.
Everything else is just biomedical
waste, RFID tags, and packing peanuts,
but you should always keep in mind
that desire is weak and easily
crowded out by fantasies
that imitate it. But where
fantasies are insistent

and promise you the world,
desire is persistent
because there is no cure for it.
And only you can know what it means,
so feel free to sniff at experts,
but that doesn't guarantee that you
will always know where to find it
and never without a doubt,
that's for certain. You need
other people for that, or
rather, because there are other people,
you can't help but find how your
desire differs. It's
a "physician, heal thyself"
kind of thing, except that it's
the healing touch that's sick,
inching towards a pinch.
So desire is your unique defect,
unique only because only you can have it,
and you can never give it away to
another person, neither can you
adopt theirs, no matter how much
pleasure it seems to give them,
you can only find it with them,
in their presence, you can use
their enjoyment as a clue
about your own but not as a guide,
and even then, those *them*
add up very few. "People
get what they need from a painting,"
Martin wrote, "the painter need

not die because of responsibility." So
on the one hand, there's the work,
which is based in the artist's
interpretation of their desire,
and then there's the painting to which
the observer's desire draws them,
and these two never overlap.
Wilde said something similar
in his essay, "The Artist as Critic,"
"It is rather the beholder who
lends to the beautiful thing its
myriad meanings, and makes it
marvellous for us, and sets it in
some new relation to the age,
so that it becomes a vital
portion of our lives, and a
symbol of what we pray for,
or perhaps of what, having prayed
for, we fear that we may receive."
What makes desire so frightening
is that you can't get rid of it,
but once you get ahold of it,
as said by one who's carried on
a wind without reprieve,
you cannot trust it to remain,
and so you make it wait.

Needless to say, my museum-going
experiences are far from reassuring.
Discharged into the gift shop,
I am, like a hillbilly at a science

fair, always unsure of what
I've come away with. When Martin writes
that the observer makes the painting,
she's saying that we never just look,
we also see, and we see before
we ever start to look. And sure,
I can't really blame my anxiety
on the unsuspecting artworks
themselves, for which my immediate
reaction would likely prove
sufficiently satisfying, but my
condition as observer surely includes
this certain space that unsettles me.
The sheer volume of wall text itself
suggests that there is something
very specific that, I suppose, I am
supposed to be getting from all this art.
It's as if the entire purpose of museums
is to keep alive the supposition that
there really is something here to see,
which betrays an anxiety that
someone somewhere surely must
know what's going on, not simply so
we should not feel abandoned to
ourselves alone (anything but that)
but so we might receive the seal
of their invincibility
to indulge in cruel ranking.
We find this pattern everywhere.
We are all of us taken in
by promises of certainty, security,

and insofar as we are all
pained by our dependencies,
if smarting still just from the first,
we come to see our weaknesses
as tempting humiliation.
We pray to God for the strength to never
ever have to pray to God again.
In this way are we our own first
despisers, trimming any loose
threads begging to be tugged.
And so we all to some degree
have built our personalities
on the mistaken presumption
that it is other people who
come along to spoil our fun.

Visiting a museum by myself—
jostled by strangers as we all
bounce between the works or
moving on just before
we get bored or become infuriated
with one another or with
the works themselves or both,
or before we have stood
in one spot before a painting
for too long a time
just because it was hard-won—
instead of art, all I see
are openings in the throng
of dawdling bodies and strategic
vantage points to be secured.

This is why, for me, it's best
to go to see art with someone I
want to talk to,
in which case the art
is just a pretense for
a conversation I'd like to have
into which individual artworks
politely insert themselves,
offering distractions like
passed hors d'oeuvres at a cocktail party,
which are brought out only to keep
the conversation off balance. Art
in this case is saved
from having to be work and can
instead be decoration—not in
the sense of being merely accidental
but ornamental in the sense of "order."

I prefer to look at art out of
the corner of my eye
while listening intently to
someone or to view
it partially behind their head
as we are talking. Don't
you find it overwhelming to
look someone in the eye the
entire time they are talking to you?
Though if you look at them
without making eye contact,
that can be awkward or
confusing for them,

so it's nice
to have art near at hand
on which to rest
your attention now and again.
And it makes a gallery or museum
a great place to take a date.
Watching someone look at art
is a good way to tell if you
will get along with them.
I think back to those first days in
North Carolina, watching
your mother in a sculpture park
turn away from a big Vollis
Simpson whirligig to comment on
a white-breasted nuthatch
bobbing through space.

It's not like I was born with a hole
in my heart the shape of your mother.
Growing up, destiny was at once
what I desperately wanted and
what I was terrified of getting.
You can't love fate
if fate turns out
to be what you
are fated to love.
"If you live by inspiration," Martin said,
"then you do what comes to you,
you can't live the moral life,
you have to obey destiny,
you can't make promises."

What she might have meant, I think,
is that you have to become the thing
that destiny would have picked
so that there can be destiny at all,
and there has to be destiny,
because while you have to do
some of the work,
you certainly can't do it all.
You can only say so much
about any one thing, because saying
is its own kind of thing.
Art is whatever you have to turn
away from, turning instead toward a bird
in space or to study a new love's
unique forms of continuity in time.
Otherwise it's just pictures of stuff.

An augur taking auspices
in ancient Rome, would only do so
from a square patch of earth
set apart for such a purpose,
called a *templum,* (from a root
that means "to cut"). I imagine
a square like Albers's homages
or even the bare canvas itself
(an alternative root suggests
something stretched). The
predictions that you get depend
on the vantages you pick,
as do those that you don't get.
Your mother was a bird that came

into view when I adjusted my frame.
Nothing magical, just another
animal stuck to this earth because
they too don't quite belong here.
It could have been anybody.
I could have been anybody.
The point is that it was us, then.
People back into destiny or step in it
accidentally on purpose, like
a cat nonchalantly tripping
on its catnip mouse. We desire
to have always loved this one,
so we forget that it was we
who invented such comeliness
in the first place. We love
so that we can forget that
it is all our fault. We love
so that the arbitrariness of
our love will not invalidate it.
And everyday, lovers choose again
to forget that their intertwined fates
are nothing more than yesses said
in the throes of infatuation, and
they shore up their yesses across time
with shared appliances and furniture,
shared beds and bank accounts,
and souvenirs that have
an equal claim on both of them,
with the goal of making it seem
like the other has been there all along,
that thankfully it's not all resting on

an uncharacteristic enthusiasm
that for a moment in the past
overwhelmed the two of them,
because if they were conscious of
that fact they would go mad,
as Freud said, "in the last resort
we must begin to love
in order not to fall ill." The weekend
your mother and I met, she lost
her fingertip cutting kale,
and we spent the better part of
the evening in the ER, surrounded by
bloodied Chux, with curling wisps
of lunar caustic floating up
from the wounded nail bed.
Her pointer finger even now,
years later, remains disfigured
and, no longer round,
comes to a point instead.

*

Near the end of our tour of New Mexico,
we took a trip to Walter
de Maria's *Lightning Field,*
which we could only reach by being
driven out into the desert
in a big black Suburban, and
there shared a cabin with a pair
of baby boomers and a couple
much younger than your mom and I

who were clean and beautiful
and as charming as a headdress
at Coachella. The back door
of the cabin opened onto a porch
that overlooked *The Lightning Field,*
which began about a hundred feet out,
though at that time of day, early
afternoon, the rods were nearly invisible
against the uniform sky. The landscape
was mostly flat. To the east a ridge
ran along the horizon. A lone black knob
rose up on the western horizon. Across
from the porch, starting about thirty feet out,
the artwork stretched south for a kilometer.
On the far side of the artwork
a nearly unnoticeable fence divided
this property from another,
and on the other side of the fence
stood an old wooden windmill
that appeared nonfunctional. Besides
the cabin and the four hundred steel rods,
the windmill was the only human-made
structure in view. It wasn't part
of the artwork, obviously.
Nevertheless, there it was,
directly in the line of sight from the porch.

Soon after arriving, it
became clear that neither couple
really knew much if anything about
the work or had any interest in

de Maria or land art in general.
Certainly, I'm no expert.
Really, I'm even a little dilettantish
about most things, especially art,
but we got the feeling, your mother and I,
that these four were here because
they'd heard about it at a party or read
about it in an in-flight magazine.
This was especially true of
the older man, who held forth
unselfconsciously about
the cost-benefit ratio of
de Maria's exacting standards for
the production and installation
of each rod, which were
replaced with some frequency
when the cumulative effects of
lightning strikes became apparent.
The older man said things like,
"From an engineering perspective...."
and "....more bang for your buck...."
dismissing as gratuitous
de Maria's instructions to
keep the discrepancy in
the relative height of each pole
to less than one one-hundredth of an inch,
as if the piece was nothing more than
the visual information that could be
gathered from the cabin's porch
by the human eye with its
relative lack of acuity. Had he

come with your mother and I
that autumn to the Guggenheim
and stood before *Untitled, 2004,*
we'd certainly have heard how he
"could have painted that."
Martin wrote, no doubt sardonically,
that the "ideal in America
is the natural man,
the conqueror, the one who can
accumulate." But really all we get
are spoilsports full of passionate
asininity. Even months
later, standing in front of
a huge Clyfford Still painting
in the Whitney, I could hear his voice,
the voice, perhaps, of a generation,
saying, "Yeah, I don't get it."

Agnes, listen!
There are ways of thinking about
the world that are, if not more useful,
then certainly less vindictive
than "getting it." The faculty
of judgement has its uses, is
unavoidable even,
but at heart it's an
apocalyptic stubbornness.
It wants for a nail when a tack would do.
The world resists our dissections,
never giving up its vital spark,
and so remains a threat against

which even the most trivial
mastery is violently pressed.
"Nature loves to hide," Heraclitus
is supposed to have said,
and in hiding itself is
thus not what is hidden. That's
what nature is, just that which
in being totally exposed
is thus never with a flourish revealed.
The trick of knowledge is that it's
ignorant of this basic tendency,
which is why we can know
anything at all, and which
is why the boomer's fallback position
was to avoid thinking, that is,
to avoid looking stupid, at all costs,
his dad jokes basing their no-need-to-know
on *Newsweek* infobites gleaned gateside.

Artworks like Martin's
and Still's can remind us
that it's okay to give yourself
over to ignorance,
unjustifiable enthusiasm,
and restless contemplation,
as long as you don't try to turn
them into wondrous signs.
The imperceptible range of
allowable discrepancies
in the relative height
of de Maria's lightning rods

doesn't appear in the work.
It's meaningful for those maintaining
the site, but for us, equipped only
with our dull senses and poor memories,
the work's spatial uniformity instead
means there is no ratio between
the rods and the uneven terrain,
no common measure. Each rod
references each other rod and nothing
else, a blanket of four-hundred points
slowly undulating across the decades
as one-by-one the rods are replaced,
a reference point continually
shifting by a hundredth of an inch.
Either the earth appears or
the artwork, never both at the same time.
They intersect without touching. Which means
that *The Lightning Field*
is a durational work in sculptural form
or a spatial work divided
by a time that does not flow,
and that by having refused to
form nature, to shape clay or marble,
nature is left to its isolation,
rising up only as the attenuation of sense.
It must have been this threat of vanishing,
of withering mastery, that spurred
the boomer's dismissive chattering,
which in time seemed to calm him,
as he trailed off finally
when no one engaged him, which

he must have taken as assent.

*

"If you don't like chaos," Martin
wrote, "you're a classicist,"
as she considered herself to be.
The post–New York consonance
where the vertical has vanished
and where thin, horizontal graphite
lines mark a clear boundary
between color fields
such that the tension between
the two is at a minimum,
is a compromise but not a solution.
Is the final painting then
a return to or of the tension
of the early work?
Glimcher compares it,
not without reason,
to *Trumpet*, from 1967,
one of the last
paintings completed
before her break,
a penciled grid
over a light gray field
whose brushstrokes
while linear are,
similarly to those in
Untitled, 2004,
unevenly applied. And there

is something about the rash
of flat black geometric shapes
in the very late canvases
that harkens back to the 1950s,
but in the final work, one sees
no tension, no unresolvable
antagonism. Certainly
a kind of disorder reminiscent
of paintings made in the '50s
and '60s has resurfaced from
a long suppression,
but this disorder is no longer one
opposed to or contrasted with order.
The peace achieved between line
and stroke has failed or is revealed
to have been illusory all along.
What returns in this last painting
is not something that had ever been
present in her work before.
The central field of dark gray
is a single (if messy) band
bisected by a penciled line
that appears to have been
drawn in after the fact, a vain
gesture immortalized. The paint
does not "fill in" the space between
the lines, as it had in all other
paintings of the later period,
when the paint strokes paralleled
the pencil. Instead, we seem to have
returned to the relative

independence of line
and color field. But not quite.
We are not witnessing here,
in this last work, the resurgence
of a chaotic swathe of strokes
overlaid with
the organizing rigidity
of the ruled line.
We can also speculate
from the fact
that the graphite lines appear
to have been drawn on
over the paint,
unlike in the video where
her brush hugs the thin line,
that the fields of dark
and light gray had
already organized themselves
into roughly rectangular bands
without the prior delineating
order of the line.
Thus it's not tension that
returns, but something
else, something that either
went unnoticed the first time round
or was never there to begin with.

Martin's paintings,
both early and late,
are continual attempts
to move from chaos

into a higher order
of perfection.
"To a detached person,"
she wrote, "the complication
of the involved life
is like chaos."
Detached people,
which Martin called "classicists,"
are those who "look out
with their back to the world,"
unlike "romanticists"
who like the chaos
of the involved life.
For classicists, like Martin,
the chaotic order of the
involved life is insufficient,
"you can't live the inspired life
and live the conventions."
Classicism "represents something
that isn't possible in the world.
More perfection
than is possible in the world."
The antagonisms between
chaos and order,
rectangle and square,
inspiration and convention, are
negated in her work
by what she calls
"the awareness of perfection,"
an order that is
not merely the opposite

of disorder but exists
without relation to disorder.

But if this is so, *Untitled,*
2004 marks the abandonment
or failure of that project
insofar as order is
no longer independent of
chaos and dissonance but is
in the end their culmination.
It's as if this final work
turns against the idea of
perfect order, which resolved
the tension of the early works
into the stable balance of
the later ones. The detachment
of "classicism," taken to
its logical end, makes it so
order is never without chaos
to the point where you
can't tell them apart.
The poisonous hope of order is
what the final painting silently
undoes, an antidote that works
by killing the patient
faster than the poison would.
It hints that the reign of order is
not established over
and above the undisciplined
and unruly but instead
arises from it,

from its unruliness,
a collusion all along.
The wildly running
washes of gray
appear to have formed
themselves into bands
which the pencil lines
merely trace, but this
order out of chaos
is not disorder's order (i.e.,
the counter-rule of chaos)
but order plain and simple,
a new classicism.

It's possible that Glimcher's story
about retrieving this last painting
and destroying two others is a lie.
Or maybe Martin had wanted this one
destroyed because of its flaw, but
Glimcher instead mistakenly
destroyed one she'd wanted to save.
Maybe Martin did love the painting,
and the splotch occurred after her death.
Or maybe the splotch rather than
an imperfection is
instead what Martin called,
"a hint of perfection,"
the slightest presence of which
makes the artwork "alive." How would
"more perfection than is possible
in the world" appear except

as a formless blot?
Why shouldn't art reserve
the privilege of putting
imperfection in
its service, or better yet,
putting itself in the service
of imperfection? What use
all these beautiful forms
and exacting proportions,
a lifetime of meticulous devotion,
if not to make the slightest mistake
burn through heaven like a dying star.

*

Alone among the rods
of de Maria's work,
which are spaced farther apart
than I'd expected them to be,
I had as spiritual of an
experience as I can have,
one not unrelated to
the arid plainness of an artwork
that is exhausted in a glance.
Maybe the lightning strikes
are really spectacular,
but ninety-nine percent of the time,
the artwork's just a bunch of poles
spaced far enough apart
nearly not to form a whole.
There was little else to do

but walk between the rods,
the sparseness of the work prompting
disengagement, distraction,
even boredom, compounded by
the fact that we'd been stranded there.
A bored distractedness that in
contrast to total absorption
describes the experience of
nature minus culture's distinction.
The poles of *The Lightning Field*
hold off the collapse of
heaven and earth, opening
up a time neither before
nor after, a place where things go
to disappear and a way for letting things
not be, not come to pass,
to just miss taking place.

Agnes,
there is no God, but God is real.
People think that throwing off
the mantle of a religious
tradition is as simple as
throwing off a mantle (which
is a kind of cloak), or that by
sheer will they can erase
even a few decades
of recent history and merrily be
the as-yet-unspecified potential
for making purchases
from the rotating

display case next to the register,
as if history is something you can
say "No" to without thereby
having always said "Yes" to it.
The only alternative to tradition
is bad tradition. This is just to say,
you are not a *tabula rasa,*
you're a mystic writing pad.
You can't help but come from somewhere,
but where you come from determines nothing.
Any beginning is a kind of lie,
what Plato called *gennaion pseudos,*
a "lie of noble birth."
A beginning always covers for
an ignoble origin, which only is
ignoble because it is deceitful,
but the truth this lie hides
is not *the* truth but just the truth
that this truth is a lie,
so that dispelling this falsehood
dispels the truth of its truth.

Take, for instance, the *Torah,*
what some call anachronistically
The Old Testament, which
begins not with *aleph (א, a)*
but *bet (ב, b): bereisheet,* "in the beginning,"
an unremarkable fact notable only
for the intimacy in Jewish
theology between Hebrew
and God's creative power. To explain

this apparent mistake, a midrash
on *Genesis* appeals to the shape
of the letter *bet* itself,
a square missing its left side,
saying that, "Just as a *bet* is closed
on all sides and open in the front,
so you are not permitted to say,
'What is beneath? What is above?
What came before?'"
The *bet* is a kind of opening bracket,
and we are living in
its parenthesis, and the *aleph,*
the whence of the *bet,* is a mystery
that cannot even be addressed
as such. How could the book
even begin with an *aleph?*
Genesis is a history
that doesn't have a history.

The second word, *bará,* which is
usually translated as "created,"
is really closer in meaning to "separated"
(related as it is to *brith,* circumcision).
Among *bará's* cognates we find
words for carving letters
in stone, separating wheat
from chaff, and refining metals.
The creation story is itself
a series of divisions: light
and darkness, water and dry land,
day and night, sun and moon,

swimming and flying creatures, God
and man, man and woman. All of this
implies that the universe was formed
by dividing up what was already there,
an activity linked to an ancient
conception of the role of deities,
which was not that of creating
but of organizing what already
exists and thereby controlling fate.
For instance, the Greek word
daimon, a tutelary spirit,
means "dispenser" and comes from
a root meaning "cut" or "divide,"
or take the Old English poem,
"The Fortunes of Men," first recorded
in the tenth-century *Exeter Book*,
so still pagan enough to be
of some use to us, which
begins its conclusion, "So
the Lord Almighty allots to all men
diversely over the face of the earth,
appoints, decrees, controls their destinies."
Bará would then mean something like
ordered, apportioned, or allotted,
like the Greek word *moros*, fate,
from which Prometheus
frees humanity, which derives from
a word meaning "I receive my portion."
With that in mind, *bereisheet* can
hardly be called a beginning
in an absolute sense. But a

beginning in an absolute
sense is already an absurdity.
In his *Confessions,* Augustine gives us
his thoughts on this perennial issue,
claiming that God is "not like a craftsman
who makes one physical object
out of another." Augustine's solution
was to bring in a third term,
the Word, *Logos,* the Son of God. But
this just puts off the inevitable,
fobbing responsibility off onto
something whose inscrutability
paradoxically provides
its explanatory thrust.
The author of the midrash, Hoshaiah,
had it right when he interpreted *bet*
as meaning it's impossible
to wonder as to the time of
origination. Augustine, too,
could only say that in the light
of God's wisdom, the very force of
creation, *et inhorresco et inardesco,*
"I tremble with fear and burn with ardor."
Fear because of God's otherness
and ardor because of kinship with Him.
In place of understanding,
there is only horror and delight.

*

I love the term "illicit substance,"

maybe even more than I do
the ones that make me go,
My God, death is everywhere
constantly present,
but then make me go, OK, fine,
let it come. I was sitting
above Maya Lin's *Wavefield,*
at Storm King,
watching this tree
become a kind of evil giant
clawing at my friend
lying face down on a bench,
and then watching
those clawing fingers
become the hooves of several
galloping horses trampling him,
and I was just like, Well,
I guess those are his weird demons.
It seemed like a good thing
they were there, trying
to destroy
my oblivious friend. Meanwhile,
across the surface of
Lin's undulating hillocks, thousands
of green beak-like articulations,
like the spikes
on the sweet gum
gumballs you love to
scavenge on the playground
in fall, opened and closed.

Elsewhere, stumbling underneath
Mark di Suvero's oversized
steel-beam sculptures,
phallic only if 'phallic' means
insecure, cognate as it is
with *Blähungen,*
German for "farts."
Dominating the main overlook,
his little tyrant with arms spread wide,
enormous beam suspended between
his leglike struts, like
a statue of Pollack or Kandinsky,
swinging his brush like a big wish.

If this were a modernist poem,
that tyrant would be a character,
would dream
like the city of Paterson
or be addressed like Crane's
Brooklyn Bridge or
like Gloucester
receive mail. My friend and I
watched him from under
a bower protected from rain,
so small from where we sat,
sharing a granola square
dripping with honey,
and he came to figure something
within me, the lifeworld of that
angry little kid I was, still am,
which crystallized into

a repertoire of anticipatory behaviors
that have long-outlived
those they were devised to piss off.
Across from our little shaded spot,
there was a bunch of
new art by young artists
against climate change
(you're welcome),
and it was all so bad
and flimsy and condescending,
and it made the whole place
seem kind of depressing, like,
all this for art? The park is
right off the highway, and
it's basically a retention pond fed
by the interstate's ditch. It didn't help
that one of the eco-artworks
was an LED traffic sign
that in this context I thought
might say something like,
"Nobody has ever loved you" or
"Deez nutz," which is what
hackers make those same signs
say *in situ*,
but instead, it displayed
a set of cheesy lines like,
"Global warming at work,"
which would make a
dumb old dad chuckle,
and then it's back to *how*
many more fracking disasters till

the next season of Game of Thrones*?*

There's an art
to being an artist
which is the art
of making yourself
be seen as an artist,
and this is the thanks they get,
us actually thinking
that they're artists. It reminds me
of pictures of young
biennial participants
striking poses
in front of their works
which are themselves side lit
and slightly out of focus
like an Olan Mills backdrop.
Hey, look at me and my art,
it's such big art!
Maya Lin at least
had the foresight to put her art
down in a kind of basin
so it doesn't compete
with the mountain behind it,
which is more beautiful though
somehow less impressive,
and there are a few
relatively modest pieces
scattered around the place
that are really enjoyable,
and mostly, like Lin's, tucked away

(and mostly made by women),
but all I remember is
di Suvero's stupid steel beams,
and just by being there,
my friend and I were
to some degree condoning
his narcissism. Like,
"Good job, little buddy, that's a real big art"
And the little tyrant straddles its hillock,
sinking in on one corner,
with its arms outstretched
in a silent harumph.

We were permeated by dampness
like two Victorian orphanages,
catching glimpses of the badgers
who live in the overgrowth
carefully manicured to frame the art.
The fucking art, Agnes.
Agnes, it felt like the end of the world,
like Samuel Colman's painting,
"The Edge of Doom," hanging
in the Brooklyn Museum, in
the Beaux-Arts Court where
you run and swing and squeal,
depicting London (and the rest of
the world) destroyed by lightning
and lava—even wingèd death,
with his hourglass and scythe
is wrecked—only a carriage
and some horse felled by a bolt

hint at the fate allotted to
the human in that annihilated place.
Were we like staffage among
the carnage of monumental art,
traipsing along the edge of doom,
the site of some forgotten Babylon?
Or were we, worse, like the "scalies"
in digital architectural models,
sometimes called "people textures,"
photos of people milling about
cut and pasted among the models'
dream-like surfaces to give them
the appearance of being habitable?
A translucent .png of sweet Agnes
in mid skip to be pasted against
the poorly rendered chain link
in some demonic model of
a border concentration camp.
We said, Why aren't we making
teargas and bullets instead of art?
We shared visions of violence,
of fire and blood traded
for water and ciprofloxacin,
for a simple dwelling place
fit for human life,
a hole in which to lie and dream,
amidst the empty desert wastes
that loomed up ahead like smoke
off burning oil fields.
But some elderly visitors
toddling onto nearby buses

broke us from our reverie.
The park was empty so
close to closing time. You were
at home with you mom,
probably being your usual
living bulwark against fear
and cynicism, but I couldn't
help feeling, strolling
among the big, stupid art,
that all your potential would be
clipped by this broken culture,
by its all-consuming wish
not to know anything about anything.
Hopefully, you can find a hill
like the one above *Wavefield*
on which to watch it all burn.

*

Agnes, from the Greek, *hagios*,
meaning both holy and accursed,
pure and impure, whole and divided,
referring to what is set apart
from ordinary life. A
part of no whole, you are thus in
some sense my life's splotch, tracing it,
shaping it, midway on life's adventure
and not just the shape mortality
makes of it with its clean edge
but also what in it shrugs off
the epithets that otherwise

would cling to it like laundry, odd
or unreasonable desires,
however humble and unremarkable,
that seemingly out of nowhere
have animated me and which tie me
to that domain where I am no longer
or not yet this legal entity
with a name useful
only for bearing fault
but instead the featureless
"person of that time,"
which a (now uncertain) future might
poorly imagine must have lived
and labored and died here,
but for what reason they won't
ever really be able to say.

Dying death takes with it even
the dignity that ought to have inhered
in mere living and does so
without pride, that is,
the trace of life
that death is in turn dies.
And death, once dead,
there's no more living then.
Marcus Aurelius said,
"All is ephemeral,
both what remembers
and what is remembered."
That's how fucking sad
everything is, because

it isn't sad, because sadness dies.
When the owl in Schuyler's
poem "Korean Mums,"
which he had watched "huge
in the dusk, / circling the field,"
is killed by Robert Dash's
Airedale Terrier, Dunny Doo,
Schuyler thinks,
"I'll / soon forget it,"
and not only the owl
but also, "the garden, the breeze / in
stillness, even / the words,
Korean mums." The splotch a life
makes on time's uneven surface,
like the one in *Untitled, 2004,*
suggests nothing in particular,
no secret whose
divulgence might
recuperate its splotchiness,
transforming it into a blessed sign
of a once-living presence,
a little ash between the eyes
ready to authenticate the
meaning of life—just that
who or whatever we believed
could have reclaimed us
is no more. How to turn that
into a value though not
one that can be liquidated?
You die and some people mourn,
but then they die, and then

you're just a name
on Ancestry.com
some distant progeny tries
to project a personality onto,
and not even the holiest Mormon
can use the splotch of your name
to dereference your immortal soul.
"Not even your name will be left,"
Marcus reminds us.
Why put all this into a poem,
then? A vain project by
any definition, a festering lily,
to be Shakespearean.
If not that middle-class muddle
of truth and beauty, then what?
A paean to secure a sinecure
from some latter-day Medici?
A quire of right-on watchwords and
peacock feathers? A lament
to elicit a tear from Iron Eyes Cody?
"If you can imagine you are
a grain of sand," Martin wrote,
"you know the rock ages."
And what about the rock
as it sails through a Beamer's
windshield or cracks
a Pinkerton's
polycarbonate visor?

If life, like the refrigerator
magnet says, is full of endless

possibilities, then death
is but one and comes but once,
having in some real sense already
taken place at birth, such that
our lives reveal their meanings in
the curl of wilting petals,
bent stalks, and hunched backs.
Everything folded in half, doubled
over, returning to the earth
which un-Icarus-like we never left.
This is why, for Martin, "*art
work is so very hard*. It is
a working through disappointments
and a growing recognition
of failure to the point of defeat."
Why not take the splotch in *Untitled,
2004* as this literal point of defeat?
If fantasies of finally getting
anywhere are what keep us going,
they also poison us with blind hope
and as such only ever lead us
to outgrow them. In this way,
their falsehood is functional,
"we still go on without hope
or desire or dreams or anything."
Martin is reminding us that our
going-on doesn't depend on us.
We are snatched from oblivion
by nothing other than
the inconstant attention of others,
themselves rescued

by the attention of still other
people, on and on, without it all
existing *pour aboutir à un livre.*
"*Defeated,*" Martin suggests,
"you will perhaps wait
and be overtaken." She's asking,
what else might be possible
if the will is not steadily in
consonance with purpose. As if
to paint abdication,
the only sovereign act, required
thirty years of airy pastels,
struck into a single form
by a blow from this last piece
and from its formless splotch.

Sometimes our anxious
concern for the people
in our lives is what
drives them away, but that
is only a structural mercy
so they won't get pressed
into the service of
our miserly selves.
Maybe subjective alienation
effected by a purely aesthetic
experience has a hygienic
function, in that staring at
impenetrable paintings (like
Untitled, 2004 or *Snoopy
Sees Earth Wrapped in Sunset*

by Alma Thomas), ignoring the
redemptive political fantasies
obscenely proffered on
the wall text next to them,
affords us some protection from
the authorities of cultural
prestige and litter prevention.
"Defeat is the beginning," Martin
said. The splotch is then a kind of
reset button, an exorcism,
the domain of life minus the fear
of death and its extortive hook,
which is just to say life
swinging freely from death's pivot.

Agnes, you are the limit
its swing approaches, a zero
carved on the far side of my boundary.
I mean, you are part of me
but a part that in reaching back
fails to find me, and I am part of you
but not the part of me
that wants to live forever.
You inevitably go on being
your own thing, buffeted by desires
both public and private, lured by
some obscure demiurge that
bubbles to the surface now and then
apparently to refind there its
motive force in a Chicken McNugget
or a Barbie doll, fully exhaustible

in their premeditated consumption,
only to see how desire remaps itself
with the intensity of its original
weirdness onto the peculiar shape
of a particular nugget or onto
some miniature plastic accessory
liberated from the doll, renewing
to some extent what consumption usurped.
The eccentric pleasures and aversions
that secrete themselves within you are
an endless source of disengagement
from the shrewd devices of
all-pervasive advertising, which
will offer up an endless series of
possessions as panaceas
to the disease of simply not possessing them.
You can always go back
and look at a painting by Martin or
by Thomas or Still
to reset the distance between yourself
and the possible future selves
spit out by nefarious algorithms as
satisfied, happy, finally enjoying
life despite common side effects,
moisturized, health conscious,
and money saving, Agnes the plucky
mom, stuffy-headed Agnes
with a big, important meeting
in the morning, Agnes who made
the smart choice for retirement,
Agnes who is adored by her

cat for choosing Meow Mix.
What I want for you is only that
you keep a practical distance
between yourself and your
identifications. It's easier that way
to hold onto them and keeps you
not only from becoming
a boring enthusiast but also and,
more importantly, from thinking
that your commitments immunize you
to the charms of a broken culture.
Truly, "fate is kind," as Martin said,
but it's not enough to leave it at that.
Knowing you're screwed either way
is just the first step toward
that Archimedean point on which
the future teeters and which is reached
only by first denying it exists.

*

Similarly to Augustine's *Confessions,*
The Zohar, written in Aramaic
in the twelfth century, seeks
to explain how a beginning begins
(a beginning that is not merely
the obverse of an end),
and one way it does this is to read
bereisheet, as *bará sheet,*
"[he] created six" (*sheet*
is "six" in Aramaic),

referring to the six days of creation
as an act without an explicit agent.
It also notes how of the ten
emanations of the infinite divinity,
the lower seven, which were
produced (*bará*) by the upper three,
were originally only six (*sheet*).
The sixth emanation, *Tiferet*,
emerged originally as a Janus-faced
hermaphrodite, only later
splitting in two so that it could
turn back toward itself.
Tiferet and its sororal twin,
Malkuth, are sometimes referred to
as "heaven" and "earth,"
and the way God created heaven and earth,
Augustine reminds us, is "not
that you made them either
in heaven or on earth." The
three highest emanations,
Keter, Hokhmah, and *Binah*,
describe a dialectic of the void
voiding itself, and *Binah*, whose
root *biyn* means to discern (as in,
to separate), reflects and refracts
the incomprehensible splendor
of *Hokhmah* shining invisibly—
eliciting horror and ardor—in the void
of *Keter*. *Binah* is, to borrow a
metaphor from a rabbi I know,
the cool surface on which the divine

essence condenses.
Of course, this also just defers
the question of origin, but
it makes of origin an irrational
spasm of God's nonexistence
(the "he" implicit in *bará sheet* is
what grammarians call a null subject).
It is at this point that we can begin
to understand the syntax
of the beginning as such, which is not
Élohim bará (God created) but *bará Élohim.*
As a plural noun, *Élohim* cannot be
the subject of *bará,* a singular verb
(though it often is when referring
throughout *Genesis* to the Judaic God).
The true subject of *bará* is unspeakable
nonsense—not even *aleph's* throaty pause
but the silent gathering of breath behind
pursed lips before *bet* is spat out.
Standing in for the unformed, *bet* appears
only as a mistake, a stain, a splotch,
which in its silence gives itself
over to the endless clash of interpretations.

Returning to one possible reading
of *bará* as purification, we might
translate, *bereisheet bará Élohim,*
as, "the gods were purified," meaning
the reduction of *Élohim* to *El,* of gods to God.
The *bará* of destinal allotment
becomes that of purgative dominance,

and gods as merely powerful give way
to an all-powerful creator-god.
Bereisheet would then name the unfixable
moment when centuries of Mesopotamian
syncretism gave way to monotheism,
in which a single god, called *Yahweh*,
a deity imported from the lands
of Edom and Midian, south
of the Kingdom of Judah,
won out over the pantheon
of Canaanite deities which
the ancient Israelites had
worshipped, which is why God in
the second creation narrative,
(*Genesis 2:4–2:25*),
is no longer referred to as *Élohim*,
"gods," but as the singular *Yahweh*,
"I am what I am, that I am, and I cause."
Bereisheet bará Élohim means,
"Don't ask how the sausage is made."

If, indignant, Roy Batty
demanded to know,
"How much blood and horror
is at the bottom of all 'good things',"
he would be told, "There is no document
of civilization which is not at
the same time a document
of barbarism." *The Book
of Joshua* details the genocide
of indigenous Canaanites,

their cities coming under *herem,*
meaning both "to destroy" and
"to devote," to consign something to God,
that to which God's law applies
only insofar as it excludes it.
The Siege of Jerusalem,
a fourteenth-century pseudo-
history of the destruction
of the Second Temple, is
as whiggish as it is anti-Semitic.
This poem, *Untitled, 2004,*
as well belongs to the verso
of history's red-marbled recto.
In any founding act, the law
of what is founded reaches into its
prehistory, which it can do
only by means of a figure covered
but not secured by the law,
suspended in a threshold of
indistinction and passage from
nature into civilization with its arts
(of rule, of love, of war), where law
discovers itself already in nature
and thus originally illegitimate
and illegitimately original,
but in the same move, nature lends
its indefinition to law.
The foundation is thus not an event
achieved once and for all
but is continually operative.

An origin is simply that which you
are prohibited from inquiring into,
not by force or by design
but because the origin distorts time,
a knot that traveled
unravels the time it takes.
The creator rearranging the world
to cover its tracks
for having rearranged the world
to cover its tracks,
tampering with the evidence
of evidence tampering. If
the ancient Israelites
had acknowledged their debt
to the lands south of Judah,
how could they also have claimed
election by the one true God?
The Canaanites were witnesses
to a version of manifest destiny,
like the Puebloans and Jicarilla
Apache were and still are.

Every phenomenal field
occludes its cause,
but only if the arbitrary
prestige of being number one,
of being naive and navelless Adam,
is of primary value.
However, Eve
in her disobedience
called out this sleight of hand,

and maybe that's what
the knowledge of
good and evil is,
to expose as forgery
all pedigree.
Even Martin knew that,
when she said, thinking
of Eve's ingurgitation,
"When you give up the
idea of right and wrong
you don't get anything.
What you do is get rid
of everything."
This was Eve's indulgence
and why her name denotes
the time prior to the first day.

*

How can I explain to you
the ambivalence
that came over me, wandering
back to the cabin after a good
romp through de Maria's folly?
Despite whatever weak mystical
experience I could forge from
my time in *The Lightning Field,*
I couldn't wriggle my way out of
the sneaking feeling that I'd bought
a pig in a poke and that the only
authentic possession I could take

away from this experience
was the privilege of saying
I'd been there,
which is what I'm doing now,
and this means that I am no
better than the boomer who
I'd viewed down the side
of my nose and whose
experience of the artwork,
with this in mind, was maybe
the more authentic one.

What was interesting about the site,
considering the work had failed
to become even a ruin, was
the amount of animal scat
between the evenly spaced
steel rods: enormous brown
pellet mounds, dried patties,
cracked logs in the low scrub.
Certainly no more concentrated here
than in the land adjacent to the artwork,
these markers of an unseen
animal presence were drawn
together and ennobled by
the mile-by-kilometer frame
de Maria's piece made in the desert,
drawn together toward a possible
meaning, the possibility of meaning.
But they also gestured to the silliness
of whatever meaning that might be

and to a natural indifference
that made the artwork's implicit
aesthetic argument, formed simply
by virtue of its having been
erected in this desert waste,
seem ridiculous. And it is,
and that is maybe its success.
It makes you feel foolish for
paying to sleep in proximity to
a single artwork, but at the
same time, it consoles you with
a vision of nature at its most dully
indifferent. Not the romantic sublime
of the raging storm but
the unobtrusive silence
of both predator and prey,
which even the keenest ear misses.
As much as nature is exhausted by
its display, it is hidden in plain sight,
its full exposure veiling it, hinting at
a deep interior which, like
The Lightning Field, it does not have,
and still for all that nature is
not something we ever see.

*

Though staffage is ornamental
and subordinate to the landscape,
it frames the painting from within,
inscribing within its bounds

a civilized and self-conscious exception
to senseless, anarchic nature as it
exists, according to some,
in its fallen state, de-Edenized by sin.
It's telling, then, that the popularity
of depictions of nature with staffage
rose in the period when Natural Philosophy
was just beginning to redescribe nature
as orderly and autonomous,
however passive, as if part of
a broader rearguard reaffirmation
of nature's lawlessness, and waned
as Romantic thought was starting
to reimagine nature as active
and creative, such that by the
twentieth century, painters
could drop figures from
their landscapes altogether.

"Homo mensura can't do without
staffage," says Beckett's Molloy,
leaning against a doorway, looking
out into the rain.
Staffage sets within the scene
a point from which the eye sets out,
takes its measure and returns,
distinguishing figure and ground.
Without it, the eye wanders aimlessly,
like Molloy himself, unsure
of where to place the accent
that might crystallize the work into

something with a beginning,
middle, and (please, God) an end.
The frame sets off the canvas from
what surrounds it, as the
inversion of our gaze. Staffage
instead frames nature, subtracting
itself by its addition, creating
within the painting a scale that
manifests distinctions between
otherwise equivalent elements.
Without staffage, no nature.

Yet in its subordinate placement,
staffage imports into the painting
what about nature is unstable,
unstageable even:
its denial of every end,
its caustic autoimmunity.
The depiction of nature in
landscape painting
finds its place in the eccentric trace
of what is not it—the human,
the domestic, the hinted-at interior,
as well as those illiterate
shepherd-poets off to the side,
bush-hid couples engaged
in the cultivated postponement
of brute coitus by ambiguous gesture,
half-wild hermits and hunters
eking out on the edge of civilization,
these afterimages of bestial nature

flaring up in a final, tragic
defense against domestication.
And even nature in its guise
as tragedy is well within
the frame that makes it legible at all.
The frame apportions nothing.
Its tight fist defines no Eden.
Instead, it marks self-possession's
scandal at what it really grasps.
Without the frame's *templum,*
nothing and everything coincide.
Heaven and earth collapse.
Staffage stuffs up this crack that
runs perpendicular to the border
separating nature and culture, and
like Prometheus, it causes us
to cease to foresee doom. We get
blind hope, instead, and in the space
opened by our ignorance,
there is something like history.

And so nature appears only
in memory, only after having
passed through it, as in
the Reverend Gilpin's carriage,
or in those vacation photos that best
replicate its utter featurelessness
in that what they capture is
only our disinterest in
ever looking at them again
and so manage all the more

to represent nature. By
neglecting the pictures we take,
we remember nature as
it really is, so when you see
some tourist in the wild
holding a black mirror between
their face and the view
or holding it with arms outstretched
to capture a landscape eclipsed
by their sunscreen-smeared faces,
feel free to dismiss any
grumblings you hear
along the lines of why can't people
just be in the present and why
do people always have to view
everything through their screens?
Tell them that the camera
frees us to forget,
which is how we honor nature.
And since its state of formlessness
is in fact the lie of art, far
from trying to substitute
itself for the real thing,
art manages only to represent
nature as unrepresentable,
a continuous surface without focus,
which in turn paints art as autonomous,
transcendent over basest stuff,
as the painted veil that mesmerizes
the impatient human, and so
nature loves to hide itself after all

but only under art's pretention.
In his *Metamorphoses,*
Ovid describes Diana's grove
as an artwork that nature has made,
writing of its stony archway
that nature had "by its own power
simulated art," suggesting,
perhaps unintentionally,
that simulation too belongs to nature,
replicating in arch and grotto
art's own nature-simulation.
As if art, far from being
nature's rival, occurs naturally,
its rule subject to its subject's consent,
and art's portrait of nature
as simple pastoral
is really nature's self-
made moretta mask.
Already within nature is
that negativity through which
it turns back on itself,
like the splotch in Martin's last,
appearing as a mutant, as
lusus naturæ, nature at play,
as wholly itself. A narrow path or strait
gate, like Ovid's "arch of living
pumice and light tufa,"
exposing nature to its voided creche,
being turned always toward
an empty future
where reproduction is only

ever partial. Nature, like Martin's
paintings, is anti-nature, which
would make art nature at its worst.

*

We were told not to photograph
The Lightning Field. Of course,
everyone else ignored this interdiction,
but your mother and I adhered to it,
because we wanted later to forget
as much as we could, since
memories accrue value
when they are exposed to loss,
and a picture just masks the loss,
so all we remember is the image.
That there was almost nothing there
to photograph is beside the point.
Your mother had by that point
somehow hurt her ankle
and so was confined to the cabin's
back porch, overlooking the artwork,
spotting birds while I walked
through the field, navigating
the thick scrub and sundry piles
of animal shit, depressions
of cracked and still-wet mud.
The steel poles were wide and solid.
I pressed my ear to one to sample
a little translated wind. Four hundred
round poles, gray and bare and in a grid.

Each tall and of a port in air,
a purified orchard, an homage to
Great Plains high-tension towers
or to the AM/FM dial, a replica in
three dimensions of centimeters
and their fractions along a ruler,
a temple cut from air. It gives
the sense of being unfinished or under
construction—skeletal, provisional.

Throughout the day, your mother and I
made nice with the older couple
and watched a family of bunnies appear
and disappear under the porch.
As evening approached,
the young couple, who had earlier
wandered off into the distance,
returned. They seem to me
in retrospect to have radiated
a pleasure that my critical
dismissiveness, however correctly
it charted their immense privilege,
had ruled suspect at the time but
which now seems unassailable,
though likely just the aftereffects
of mushrooms and some sort of
fringed and beaded eco-eroticism.
As the sun set, the rods stood out
against the dimming landscape,
their western edges
glowing while

the eastern sides cooled.
Your mother
climbed on my back,
and I walked us
a couple rows deep
and spread out a
blanket in the dirt
so she could get away
from the cabin
and into the field
as night came on.

*

Sometime after having finished
what would become her last painting,
Martin made a drawing,
also her last, a few inches in size,
of a potted plant, which also has
the name *Untitled, 2004*.
Representational, the drawing seems
unprecedented in Martin's career.
A thin, unbroken line traces
the basic shape of leaves and vessel,
like a blind-contour drawing.
The line wavers, seems little more
than the record of a spasm.
A second, much shorter line
starts in the midst of the leaves,
moving vertically, unsteadily,
then loops back on itself,

suggestive of a stem and a bud,
which if drawn from life
she would never see bloom.

We come to life as the fruit
of some gone blossom
and depart as the seed
for some flower yet to bloom.
While the blossom buds forth,
the leaves that prepared the blossom
now fall off. The fruit comes to light,
while the blossom disappears.
This means that to live is
to follow a path that in
making its way makes way
and makes a way for that
which doesn't know it waits to be,
however impatiently,
and our mighty works fail to flower
if they don't contain within themselves
the germ of their own corruption.
A splotch, you might say. That's how
the flower appears to
the ripening fruit, the fruit
to the still-closed bud.
The future is before all else
yet to be. The next day,
we all watched as
a snake slithered under
the desert cabin's porch.

The image of achieved perfection
can only take the form of a mistake,
so our might and purity will be
realized in its undoing.
The splotch in Martin's painting,
which now looks to me
like a flower pressed
to wet paint, is the equivalent
of the bud in her final drawing,
which rises like a little balloon
tied to its own separate line,
the same way death tracks a line
perpendicular to that of the life
that it completes by interrupting it,
putting all this stuff, all these
corpuscles writing to you,
on another trajectory. No one
can follow that line, just as
your mother and I can't follow you,
dear Agnes. As you bud forth, we
wither away, as the worm's
dying skin is the cradle
of its metamorphosis.

Wherever the splotch appears
it should be named as such.
Celan has a line that goes, "the name
guilds the feints." It means,
a word is not a stand-in but instead
is the ruse behind which what
is named is able to escape.

The name adorns a vacancy,
a vanity, and doing so
imports this dupery, unites
us to the world as fool to knave.
We are not argued but seduced
into existence, we suffer into
being, and everything
else just gilds that fact, although
more oft than not as disavowal
of what the name in failing therefore names.
But even then, the mad desire
to master and possess nature,
to ground what is on ground that is
not ash and dust, bears a trace
of first dependency ill met.

Agnes, I know almost nothing,
and it has taken me nearly
forty years to learn how dumb
I've always been. So what advice
could I give you about
making your way in a world
that as I write is being
manufactured expressly
to be unfit for human life?
Any advice would outdate
upon the lips. But what you must
bear, you will, because you are
already perfectly imperfect,
and this is your strength because
it's the how and why of things

to be ad hoc and provisional.
So, if all this must boil down to
some pithy advice, let me
simply say of your peculiar
imperfection, whatever
it turns out to be, that you
should never make excuses for it,
and never should you trade
your unapologetic predilections
for the efficacy of explanations.
Defend your right to be unfinished.
Defend whatever in this life
preempts supremacy, because
life is weakness and vulnerability
and dependence, life
is mutant and improvised
and accidental, and though it
has always enlisted fear,
it yet has bred fear's opposite,
which is love, the most improbable
thing in the universe,
which no one understands and
probably does not exist,
though if it does, it will
debride your armored essence,
leaving behind a stain, which you
will have to offer others as
a vain thing to be loved, a splotch—
gray, bare, incommodious—
in which to find an endless life,
one of purpose disyoked, a

meaningless means to no end.
Love can't see farther than one
inch in front of its face.
It's useless for doing anything,
but in the end, what use are you?
What are any of us for?
Surely not for love, since love
is nothing but the mark
of our basic uselessness.
So you must let love pick apart
your composure. Why? For no
reason. Because I said so. Let
love reject all conditions,
and to the extent it fails
to live up to its own harsh demands,
it will lead you to agree
to the possibility of your
ruin and to follow as it lets
what must die pass away in peace
in order just for love to be at all.

Back at the cabin, *The Lightning Field*
lost to the night, we lay in the dirt
and watched the enormous moon set
like a face sinking into a still, black pond.
The way the top of it winked out
seemed definitive, like it
would never rise again. The stars
clamored for our attention
only to become still when our gazes
settled on them. You see,

the foveal pit in the back of the eye,
where light sharpens to a point,
can pick out the cursive wisp
of a horse's back in Turner's *Shade*
and Darkness or a faint graphite
line awash in pastels, but it just
flattens a star's flickering
into a cold, dim dot.
And now, when rocking you to sleep
in the dark of your room, you
dozing off, human on
my faithless arm, I set my gaze
on the curl of your tiny ear
to check if your eyes are closed or not.

It's like a metaphor for something,
I don't know what. It means something
like, intention destroys beauty or,
we are only ever thrilled obliquely
or, a glance lives on longer than a stare.
It means, never give them everything,
never work the full eight hours, never
learn all of the hymns or march
at all of the demos. Keep something
for yourself, a dark point
at the center of your sight,
around which everything else
can twinkle, spark, and fade,
a windmill useless and abandoned
at the edge of vision, or
a sharpened point to tempt a thunderbolt

and remain unscorched.
Martin's paintings are glances,
deflecting our gazes, and as such can never
be caught in a fixed stare. Nothing is there
that doesn't hurry the eye along,
as if something is forever catching you
out of the corner of your own eye,
remaining always at the edge
of vision as your gaze rolls
around toward it, spiraling on,
never returning to the point of its birth.

Quotations not indicated as such in the text, in the order in which they appear:

"The music of paradise is made of the continual clashing of swords"

"Nature as the production of the diverse can only be an infinite sum, that is, a sum which does not totalize its own elements"

"temples, images, and customs are no longer capable of taking on the historical vocation of a people in order to compel it in a new task"

"Moves perpetually in its stillness"

"helixes of conch-shell cores"

"To use other people's enjoyment as a clue about your own but not as a guideline or an order"

"And glad not to have invented / Such comeliness, we are surrounded"

"The only alternative to tradition is bad tradition"

"in that annihilated place," "the site of this forgotten Babylon"

"And Death once dead, there's no more dying then"

"How much blood and horror is at the bottom of all 'good things'?" (attributed in the text to Roy Batty, the cyborg antagonist from *Blade Runner*)

"There is no document of civilization which is not at the same time a document of barbarism"

"The foundation is thus not an event achieved once and for all but is continually operative"

"Every phenomenal field occludes its cause"

"Death – is but one – and comes but once"

"the process demands that, during the whole operation, the workman's will be steadily in consonance with his purpose"

"While the blossom buds forth, the leaves that prepared the blossom now fall off. The fruit comes to light, while the blossom disappears"

"But / what you must bear, you will"

"human on my faithless arm"

Acknowledgements

The author would like to thank the following people without whose comments and encouragement this work would be all the poorer: Marie Buck, who also published a section online at *Social Text*, Joe Fletcher, Rob Halpern, Lucy Ives, Ted Rees, and Steve Zultanski. Kay Gabriel provided helpful advice concerning some Ancient Greek. The rabbi with the condensation metaphor is Josh Bolton, although his metaphor wasn't specifically about *sefirot*. And though the poem is for Agnes Giffin, it is also dedicated to Laura Mauldin.

Lawrence Giffin is the author of several books of poetry, including *Plato's Closet* (Roof Books, 2016) and *Christian Name* (Ugly Duckling Presse, 2012). He is a co-editor at Golias Books.